Christmas Things to MAKE & DO

igloo

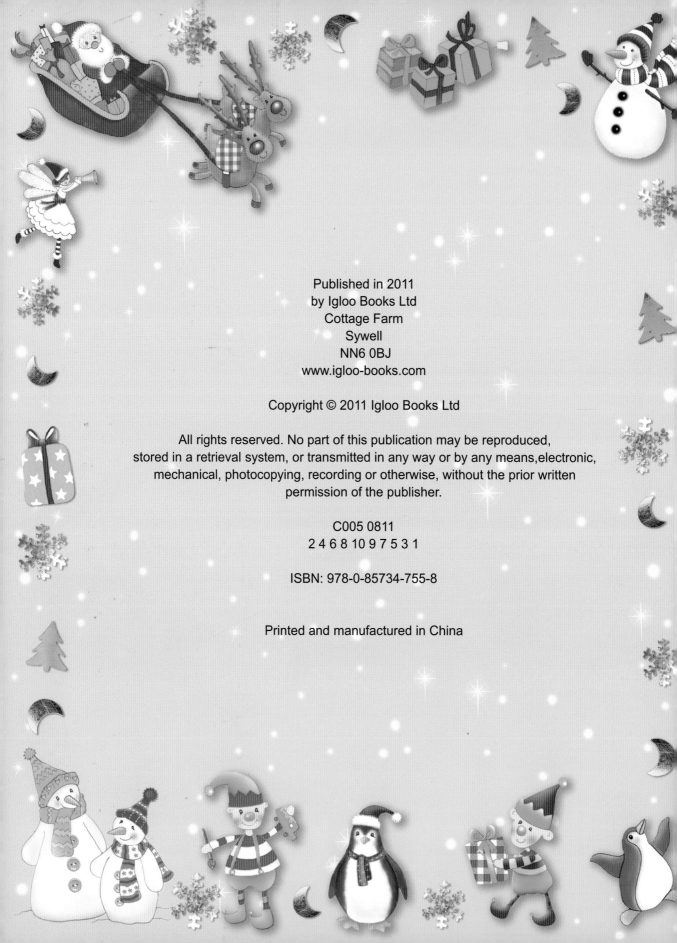

Published in 2011
by Igloo Books Ltd
Cottage Farm
Sywell
NN6 0BJ
www.igloo-books.com

C005 0811
2 4 6 8 10 9 7 5 3 1

ISBN: 978-0-85734-755-8

Printed and manufactured in China

Contents

Christmas Stocking

Make your own Christmas stocking to hang up for Santa.

You will need:

* White paper
* Pencil
* 2 pieces of red fleece for the stocking
* Green felt for holly decoration
* Red beads, or buttons, for holly berries
* Long sewing pins
* Large-eye sewing needle
* Embroidery thread
* Safety scissors
* Glue
* Tinsel to trim

Step 1: Draw a stocking shape onto a piece of white paper and cut it out. Ask an adult to help you pin the paper to the pieces of red felt and cut out 2 stocking shapes.

Step 2: From the leftover red felt, cut out a long strip for the hanging loop.

Step 3: Ask an adult to help you pin together the stocking shapes and sew the edges together, leaving the top open.

Step 4: Turn your sewn stocking inside out. Sew the loop onto the outside edge.

Step 5: Cut out some holly shapes from the green felt. Stick these onto your stocking. Sew on red beads, or buttons, for the berries.

Step 6: Stick tinsel around the open end of your stocking.

Use the loop to hang your stocking on the end of your bed.

Pretty Paper Chains

You will need:

* Bright paper, or Christmas wrapping paper
* Safety scissors
* Glue, or sticky tape

Make some pretty paper chains to decorate your tree.

Step 1: Cut out about 50 strips of bright paper, or Christmas wrapping paper. The strips should be about 2cm (¾in) wide and 12cm (4¾in) long.

Christmas Cookies

Ask an adult to help you with the first 2 steps.

Ingredients:

* 100g (4oz) butter
* 175g (6oz) light soft brown sugar
* 4 tablespoons (60ml) golden syrup
* 350g (12oz) plain flour
* 1 teaspoon (5ml) bicarbonate of soda
* 2 teaspoons (10ml) ground ginger
* 1 large egg, beaten
* grated rind of 1 lemon

To decorate:

* 65g (1.5oz) icing sugar
* 1 tablespoon (15ml) lemon juice
* sweets, or cake decorations

Step 1: Preheat the oven to gas mark 5/190°C/375°F. Grease two baking sheets.

Step 2: In a small pan, melt the butter, sugar and syrup together. Leave to cool.

Step 3: Sift the flour, soda and ginger together into a bowl. Stir the butter mixture into the flour with the egg and lemon rind to make a firm dough.

Step 2: Glue, or tape, the ends of one strip together to make a loop.

Step 4: Keep threading and gluing loops until you have made a long chain.

Step 3: Now thread a strip of paper through the first loop and make another loop.

Step 6: Mix the icing sugar and lemon juice together and spoon small blobs onto the biscuits. Stick the sweets, or cake decorations, onto this and leave to set.

Step 4: Roll out the mixture on a floured surface. Use shaped cookie cutters to press out your biscuits. Re-roll the dough as you go along.

Step 5: Put your biscuits on the baking sheets and bake for 10-12 mins, or until golden. Ask an adult to put them on a wire rack to cool.

Party Invitations

Make some festive party invites.

You will need:
* Card, folded * Safety scissors
* Crayons, or felt-tips * Glue
* Decorations such as sequins,
  wiggly eyes and ribbon

For a funny snowman invite, draw a
snowman head peeping over a wall.
Glue wiggly eyes on the snowman.
Write "See you at my party!"
on the wall.

To make a Christmas pudding invite, draw a
Christmas pudding on the front of the card. Decorate
your card with crayons, or felt-tips. Draw some holly
on green paper to stick on the top of the pudding.
Decorate with red and gold sequins.

Don't forget to write the date,
time and address of
your party inside.

To make a Christmas present invite, turn your
folded card so the fold is at the top. Decorate the
front to look like a Christmas gift. Draw on
wrapping paper and glue on some ribbon tied in
a bow.

Hidden Elves

Play this game and see who finds the most hidden elves.

You will need:

* Card, or thick paper
* Tracing paper * Pencil
* Felt-tips, or pencil crayons
* Safety scissors

Step 1: Trace 10, or more of these elves onto the card, or paper.

Step 2: Finish the elves with felt-tips, or pencil crayons, on one side.

Step 3: On the back of each elf write the numbers 1 to 10

1   10

Step 4: Hide the elves around the house.

To play the game:
Everyone has 10 minutes to find the hidden elves. Each person then adds up the numbers on the back of the elves they've found. The person with the most points is declared the winner.

Festive Paper Wreath

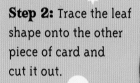

You will need:

* A piece of white card slightly bigger than a dinner plate
* A piece of white card about 4in (10cm) square
* Tracing paper * Pencil * Safety scissors
* Wrapping paper, or tissue paper, in different shades of green * Sticky tape, or glue
* Ribbon and glitter to decorate

Step 1: On the piece of card, draw round a dinner plate and then a smaller plate inside that circle to make a ring. Carefully cut it out.

Step 2: Trace the leaf shape onto the other piece of card and cut it out.

Step 3: Draw around your leaf 20 times on the wrapping, or tissue paper. Cut out all the leaves.

Step 4: Tape, or glue, each leaf to the card ring until one side is covered in leaves. Stick the rest of the leaves in the opposite direction, filling up any white areas. You may need to make more leaves.

Step 5: Decorate your wreath with a ribbon.

You can also dab glue on the leaves and sprinkle them with glitter.

It's Snowing!

Make some pretty snowflakes to decorate your tree, or to stick on cards and presents.

You will need:
* A mug, or cup * White paper * Pencil
* Safety scissors * Sequins, or glitter

Step 1: Put the mug, or cup, on top of a piece of white paper and draw round it with a pencil to make a circle.

Step 2: Cut out the circle you have drawn. Fold it in half and then fold it in half again.

Step 3: Snip out little shapes all over the folded paper.

Step 4: Open out the paper and decorate your snowflake with sequins, or glitter. Now make some more!

Christmas Strings

Make some pretty Christmas strings to decorate your home, or classroom.

You will need:
* Thick white paper, or thin card – about 3 sheets of A4
* Tracing paper * Pencil crayons, or paints * Thread, or thin ribbon

Step 1: Trace the shapes given here onto the plain paper, or card.

Step 2: Use your pencil crayons, or paints, to fill in the shapes.

Step 3: Ask an adult to make holes at the top and bottom of each shape.

Step 4: Use the thread, or ribbon, to join the shapes together to make a hanging Christmas string.

Step 5: After threading each shape, tie knots in the string to stop each shape slipping down the string.

Make a Maraca

Easy-to-make maraca for some Christmas music.

You will need:

* Two empty yogurt pots, or plastic cups, cleaned
* Small dried pasta shapes
* Glue and sticky tape
* Christmas wrapping paper
* Shiny wrapping ribbon

Step 1: Pour the pasta shapes into one cup, so it is half full.

Step 2: Glue the other cup on top. Use sticky tape around the join.

Step 3: Cover your maraca in wrapping paper. Make sure the ends are stuck down with glue, or sticky tape.

Step 4: Tie a long strip of ribbon around the middle.

Now use your maraca to play along with Christmas songs!

Snowman Pencil Top

Add this festive pencil as a stocking filler for a friend.

You will need:

✱ Pencil ✱ Craft foam in white, black, orange and red
✱ Safety scissors ✱ Wiggly eyes
✱ Glue ✱ Mini pompoms

Step 1: Cut out 2 snowman shapes from the foam.

Step 2: Glue the two shapes together around the edges leaving the bottom edge open.

Step 3: To finish the head, cut a mouth from the black foam and a nose from the orange foam. Glue these on the head. Glue on the wiggly eyes.

Step 4: To finish the body, glue on the pompoms for buttons. Cut three strips from the red foam for the scarf. Glue these on the body. Let the glue dry.

Step 5: Dab glue on the end of the pencil. Place the pencil inside the snowman. Glue the bottom edges of the snowman and press these together.

Santa's Grotto

Make a picture of Santa's grotto then tell him
what you'd like for Christmas.

You will need:

* A large sheet of paper
* Lots of other bits and
  pieces, such as sweet
  wrappers, wrapping
  paper, pasta shapes,
  rice and scraps of
  fabric
* Safety scissors
* Glue

Use your bits and
pieces to build up Santa's
grotto by sticking them onto the large
sheet of paper. Use ideas you see here
and add some of your own.
Try using cotton wool for
Santa's beard.

Snowball Piñata

Make your own snowball piñata — ask an adult to help you.

You will need:
* A small, round balloon * Lots of old newspapers torn into strips
* Paper maché paste * Bright paint * Glitter
* Sweets and small toys to fill the piñata
* String, or ribbon * Sticky tape

Step 1: Ask an adult to blow up the round balloon and tie a knot in the end.

Step 2: Dip the newspaper strips into the paper maché paste and cover the balloon with the strips, leaving a hole at the top. Let this dry.

This is messy, so wear an apron and put lots of newspaper on the table.

Step 3: Cover the balloon with another layer of newspaper and leave it to dry, too. Repeat with one more layer of newspaper, making sure you leave the hole at the top.

Step 4: When this layer is dry, ask an adult to pop the balloon and take it out.

Step 5: Paint your piñata and add some glitter. Use the hole at the top to fill your piñata with fun surprises, such as small toys and sweets.

Step 6: With a piece of string and sticky tape, attach your piñata to the ceiling, or a door hook. Hit the piñata with broom handles until it breaks and the treats inside fall out.

Toy Decorations

Decorate your tree with Christmas toys.

You will need:
* Thin card * Safety scissors
* Felt-tips, crayons, or stickers to decorate
* Thread, or ribbon, for hanging

Step 1: Copy these toy shapes onto thin card.

Step 2: Use felt-tips, crayons, or stickers, to decorate them.

Step 3: Cut out the shapes.

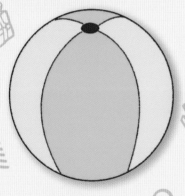

Step 4: Ask an adult to make a small hole at the top of each shape. Use thread, or thin ribbon, to hang them on the tree.

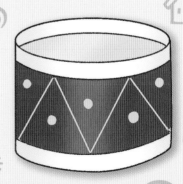

Christmas Tree Cookies

Fun to make, a treat to eat!
Ask an adult to help with the steps.

You will need;

- 110g (4oz) butter, softened
- 110g (4oz) caster sugar
- 1 large egg, beaten with 2 teaspoons of water
- 1 teaspoon vanilla extract
- 275g (9.5oz) plain flour
- Large pinch of baking powder
- Pinch of salt

To decorate:

- Ready-made icing
- Silver balls
- Hundreds and thousands

Step 1: Use a mixer, or wooden spoon, to mix the butter and sugar until the mixture is soft and creamy.

Step 2: Beat the egg and water with the vanilla extract.

Step 3: Mix with the butter and sugar.

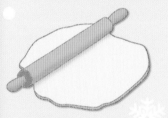

Step 4: Sift in the flour, baking powder and salt. Mix it all together until it is like a dough.

Step 5: Wrap the dough in cling film and chill in the fridge for 30 minutes. Pre-heat the oven to gas mark 4/180°C/356°F.

Step 6: Lightly flour your work surface and a rolling pin. Roll out the dough. Use a cake cutter to cut out your tree shapes.

Step 7: Place the cookies onto a lightly-greased baking tray. Bake for 10 mins. Put them on a wire rack to cool.

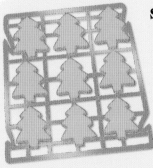

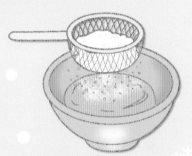

Decorate your cookie trees with icing, hundreds and thousands and silver balls.

Stand-up Santa

Make a stand-up Santa and his sack of presents for home, or school.

For one Santa you will need:
* Cardboard tube * Tracing paper * Pencil * Sheets of white paper
* Safety scissors * Glue * Pencil crayons, felt-tips, or paints
* Cotton wool * Thin card for Santa's sack

Glue

Step 1: Trace this Santa hat and tab onto white paper, or draw your own. Use your pencil crayons, felt-tips, or paints, to make the hat red on both sides. Leave the tab white. Cut it out.

Tab

Step 2: Paint your cardboard tube red. Let it dry.

Step 3: Glue the hat to the cardboard tube so that the tab is on the outside. Let the glue dry.

Step 4: Draw Santa's face on the tab. Draw buttons on his coat.

Step 5: Use the cotton wool to make Santa's beard and to finish his hat.

Step 6: To make Santa's sack, fold the card in half from top to bottom. Draw the sack onto the folded card with the top of the sack on the folded edge. Make it brown on all sides.

Step 7: Cut out the sack and stand it next to your Santa.

To use the Santa as a place name, write the person's name on the sack.

21

Advent Calendar

You will need:
* A large (A3) sheet of card
* Sheet of paper to make 24 flaps
* Felt-tips
* Sheet of 24 stickers
* Glue

Step 1: Draw a Christmas tree on the piece of card.

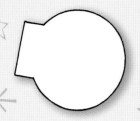

Step 2: For the flaps for your calendar, draw 24 shapes that look like Christmas baubles onto the white paper

Step 3: Cut out the shapes. Glue the tab at the top of each bauble and press each one on your tree.

Step 4: Lift the flap and draw a small picture, or add a sticker underneath.

Twisty Garlands

You will need:
* A roll of crepe paper
* Old newspaper
* Glue * Glitter
* Safety scissors

Step 1: Unroll a piece of crepe paper and cut a long strip about 5cm (2in) wide.

Step 2: Put this strip on a sheet of newspaper. Brush a line of glue along the middle of the crepe paper.

Step 3: Sprinkle the glue line with glitter and leave it to dry.

Step 5: Decorate the rest of the calendar with felt-tips and extra stickers.

Step 6: Write a number on the front of each bauble, from 1 to 24.

Open each door from 1st December up until Christmas Eve!

Step 4: When the glue is dry, make another glittery line on the other side.

Step 5: When the glue is dry, roll the crepe paper loosely around your hand and squash it.

Step 6: Snip a fringe along each edge, cutting through the whole length of crepe paper, but not through the line of glitter in the middle.

Unroll the garland and then twist it. Make more in different shades and use them to decorate a room, or Christmas tree.

Bookmark Gifts

2.5cm (1in)

Here are some ideas for Christmas bookmarks to make for yourself, or friends.

Cut out a piece of plain card. Draw a Christmas scene, or stick on pictures cut out from magazines and old Christmas cards.

15cm (6in)

You can use safety scissors to cut the end to make a tassel.

Trace one of these shapes onto a piece of thin card. Cut out the shape and fill it in to make a special festive gift.

Christmas Morning

Use this picture to make a Christmas collage.

You will need:

* Large sheet of white paper * Lots of bits of Christmas wrapping paper and plain paper in different shades
* Any scraps of fabric * Safety scissors * Glue
* Crayons, felt-tips and paints

Use the scraps of paper and fabric, crayons, felt-tips and paints to make a picture of the teddies on Christmas morning. Use this one as a guide.

Santa Picture Frame

Make a present photo frame decorated with Father Christmas.

You will need:

* A piece of thick card folded from top to bottom
* Photo
* 2 sheets of A4 plain white paper
* Pencil crayons, paints, or felt-tips
* Safety scissors * Glue

Step 1: Stick your photo in the middle of the front of the folded card.

Step 2: On one sheet of paper draw lots of small Christmas presents like this.

Step 3: Cut them out. Glue the presents around the photo so you cover all the card.

Step 4: Copy this father Christmas face onto the other sheet of white paper. Finish it and cut it out.

Step 5: Stick it on a top corner of the frame to finish.

Merry Xmas Banner

Get together with some friends to make this festive banner.

You will need:

* A long strip of paper, or several pieces taped together
* Ruler
* Pencil
* Red, or green paint
* Lots of old newspapers
* Felt-tips
* Medium-sized paintbrush
* Safety scissors

Step 1: Use a ruler to draw a line about 5cm (2in) from the top of the paper along its full length.

Step 2: From the line, draw V shapes to the bottom edge. You will need 1 V shape for each letter plus the space between the letters. So for Merry Xmas you will need 10 V shapes.

Step 3: Cut around the V shapes. Over the newspaper, paint the banner. Leave it to dry.

Step 4: Use felt-tips to write the letters in the V shape.

Finish your banner with holly decorations.

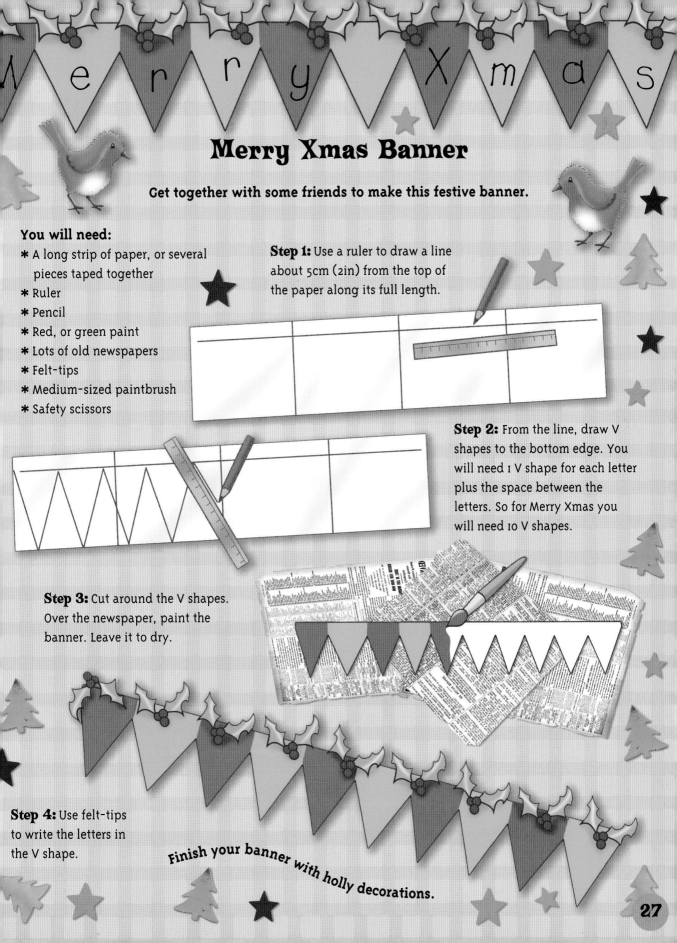

Gingerbread Men

Make a row of smiling gingerbread men.

You will need:
* Plain white paper about 38 cm (15in) long and 15 cm (6in) deep
* Safety scissors
* Pencil crayons, or felt-tips

Step 1: Fold a rectangle of white paper like this.

Step 2: Draw a gingerbread man on the front, so that the arms and feet touch the edges of the paper.

Step 3: Cut this out carefully, cutting around the shape through all the folded paper.

Step 4: Open out your chain of gingerbread men. Using pencil crayons, or felt-tips, draw their faces and clothes. Make each one look different.

You can make lots of chains and join them together to make a long wall decoration for home, or school.

Glittering Angels

Make sparkling angels to hang on your tree.

You will need:
* Tracing paper * Pencil
* Thin card * Safety scissors
* Crayons, or felt-tips
* Old newspapers * Glue
* Silver and gold glitter mixed together, or red and green glitter mixed together
* Thread, or thin ribbon

Step 1: Trace this angel onto card. Cut out the angel shape. Ask an adult to help you make a hole at the top of the shape.

Step 2: Use your crayons, or felt-tips, to finish the angel on both sides.

Step 3: Spread out some old newspapers. Cover one side of the angel with glue. Sprinkle on the glitter. When this dry, add glitter on the other side. Tie the ribbon or thread through the hole.

Make lots of angels and hang them on the tree.

Christmas Grotto Race

See who is the first to help Santa deliver all the presents and get back to the grotto.
To play, make some counters and find a die.

To make the counters you will need:

∗ Thin card –
   1 A4 sheet
∗ Tracing paper
∗ Safety scissors
∗ Pencil crayons

Trace or copy the shapes above onto the card. Crayon them in and cut them out. You will need one counter for each player.

Stop to say "ho! ho! ho!" Miss 1 turn

Sled down a hill – move on 3 squares

Join in some carol singing – miss 1 turn

Stop for a snowball fight – miss 2 turns

START

30

SANTA'S GROTTO

END

Stop for a mince pie - miss 1 turn

Whiz around the bend - move on 2 squares

Build a snowman - miss 1 turn

Start to jog - move on 2 squares

Whistle a tune - move on 2 squares

Dropped a present - miss 1 turn

Stop to watch some skaters - miss 1 turn

Sweet Sugar Mice

Make these sugar mice for a Christmas stocking treat.

For 12 mice you will need:

- I egg white
- 500g (17oz) icing sugar
- Few drops of water
- Pink, or blue, food dye
- Raisins, or small chocolate drops, for eyes
- Licorice strings

Step 1: Whisk the egg white until it is firm.

Step 2: Sift the icing sugar into the egg white and mix together.

Step 3: Add a few drops of water mixed with the food dye. Knead the mixture together to make a firm paste.

Step 4: Divide the mixture into 12 pieces. Shape each piece into a mouse with a pointed end for the nose. Pinch up two ears on the top of the head and add the eyes.

Step 5: Add the liquorice strings for the tails.

Step 6: Leave your mice for a few hours to go hard.

Stand-up Robins

These robins can be used as decorations, Christmas cards, or place names.

You will need:

* Thin card
* Tracing paper
* Pencil
* Felt-tips, or crayons
* Safety scissors

Step 1: Fold the card in half from top to bottom.

Step 2: Trace this robin, or draw your own, onto the folded card. Make sure the head and tail touch the fold.

Step 3: Use your felt-tips, or crayons, to finish the picture of the robin. Draw on some snow. Next, cut around the top half of the robin shape. Do not cut where the head and tail touch the fold.

Step 4: Open out your robin. For a card or gift tag, write your message inside. For a table place name, write the person's name on the back.

Stamp Pad Wrapping Paper

You will need:

* A large sheet, or roll, of bright, plain paper
* Gold paint
* Stamp pad and stampers

Step 1: Spread out your large sheet of paper. Add stripes, or blobs of gold paint first before stamping.

Step 2: Use your stampers and stamp pad to decorate the paper. Plan where you will stamp on your paper — it can be a random, or a regular, pattern.

Try using the stamps in different patterns on different types of paper.

Stained-glass Window

You will need:
* Pieces of tissue paper in different shades
* An A4 piece of black paper, or card

Step 1: Fold the black paper, or card in half. Draw and cut out half a shape along the folded edge. Leave some space at the top and bottom.

Glue

Step 2: Glue the pieces of tissue paper onto the black cut-out picture.

Step 3: When the glue is dry, tape your stained-glass window to a real window.

The light shining through will make it glow.

Hanging Star

Make a hanging star decoration for your Christmas tree.

You will need:

* Thin card, or thick paper
* Tracing paper
* Pencil
* Pencil crayons, or felt-tips
* Safety scissors
* Thread, or ribbon

Step 1: Trace two star shapes onto the paper, or card.

Step 2: Crayon in the shapes and cut them out.

Step 3: Make a cut in each shape as shown.

Step 4: Slide the two slits into each other to make your star decoration.

Step 5: Ask an adult to help you make a hole in the top of the star. Use thread, or ribbon, to make a loop to hang your star.

Snowman Pencil Holder

A great idea for school, home, or as a gift.

You will need:

* A clean empty jar * Large paint brush * White water-based paint for glass
* Cotton wool balls - enough to cover the jar * Glue * Small piece of black felt
* Small piece of orange felt * Wiggly eyes
* **Optional** - small knitted doll's scarf, or piece of ribbon

Step 1: Paint the outside of the jar with white paint. Let this dry.

Step 2: Glue the cotton wool balls onto the jar to cover it completely.

Step 3: From the black felt, cut out the snowman's hat and mouth. Glue these into place.

If the jar is tall enough, tie the scarf, or ribbon, round the jar to finish off your snowman.

Step 4: From the orange felt, cut out a small triangle for the snowman's nose. Glue it in place. Glue on the wiggly eyes.

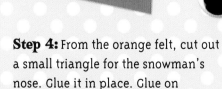

Balls in the Box

Scrunch up Christmas wrapping paper to make balls the size of a tennis ball. Find an empty box. Stand behind a line. See how many balls you can get in the box. Take it in turns to have two goes each. The first person to get 10 balls in the box is the winner.

Puppet Play

Trace and cut out these figures and then put on a play.

You will need:
* Tracing paper
* Pencil
* Thin sheets of card
* Safety scissors
* Pencil crayons, or felt-tips

Christmas Day Diary

Make a diary to keep a record of your Christmas Day.

You will need:

* 3 sheets of white A4 paper
* Pencil crayons and felt-tips
* 1 sheet of A4 that's not white, for the cover * Glue

With the non-white sheet on the outside, fold all the paper in half to make a booklet. Draw a Christmas picture on the front and write your name and the date.

Keep a record of your presents, who came to visit, what you had to eat and what games you played.

Draw pictures of your family and friends having fun, or stick in photos.

Trace the shapes onto the card. Fill them in. Cut out the shapes and ask an adult to cut out the finger holes. Put your fingers in the holes to make the figures move.

Christmas Flowers

Make these pretty, festive flowers as a gift, or decoration.

You will need:
* Green and red tissue paper ✱ Gold, or silver, pipe cleaner
* Safety scissors ✱ Newspaper ✱ Glitter ✱ Red ribbon
* **Optional** - twigs; plus silver, or gold, spray paint

Step 1: Cut 15 long strips of tissue paper about 12cmx18cm (5x7in) wide.

Step 2: Hold the strips of paper together. Fold the pile of strips like an accordion.

Step 3: Tie the pipe cleaner around the middle of the folded paper.

Step 4: Gently pull each piece of paper upwards so each sheet of paper makes a petal.

Step 5: Gently put dabs of glue on the petals. Sprinkle glitter over the flowers.

Option: Over old newspaper spray gold, or silver, paint onto your twigs.

Make several flowers and tie them together with a pretty ribbon. Add some decorated twigs for a really sparkling bunch of flowers.

Or use one flower to decorate a gift.

Snowball Cookies

Make some snowball cookies for Christmas treats.

Ingredients:
- 100g (4oz) butter (softened)
- 25g (1oz) cornflour
- 75g (3oz) plain flour
- 25g (1oz) icing sugar
- 50g (2oz) dessicated coconut

Step 1: Mix the butter with the cornflour, plain flour and icing sugar until the dough is firm.

Step 2: Divide the dough in to even amounts and roll each portion into a small ball.

Step 3: Roll each ball in the coconut.

Step 4: Place the snowballs well apart on a lined baking sheet and press down lightly with the back of a fork.

Step 5: Ask an adult to bake these at gas mark 4/180°C/356°F for 15-20 mins, until golden.

Snow Globes

Make these lovely ornaments for yourself, or as gifts.

You will need:

* Clean glass jar with a screw on lid
* Small Christmas figures such as a Santa, a snowman and miniature trees
* Florist clay * Silver glitter
* Water that has been boiled and then cooled
* Waterproof glue

Step 1: Choose the figures you want inside your globe.

Step 2: Arrange them in a small group on the inside of the lid using florist clay to keep them in place.

Step 3: Fill the jar with water leaving 2.5cm (1in) at the top. Sprinkle in a teaspoon of glitter.

Step 4: Put a layer of glue inside the rim of the lid. Place the lid on the jar so the figures are upside-down and then screw the lid on tight.

Step 5: Make sure the outside of the jar and lid are dry. Add a layer of glue around the rim of the lid to stop any water leaking out. Let the glue dry. Add tinsel around the lid to cover the join.

Mosaic Coasters

Recycle your old CDs to make these mosaic Christmas coasters for a present.

You will need:

* Old CDs
* Thick green, or red paper.
* Safety scissors
* Glue
* Green, red, gold and silver sweet wrappers

Step 1: Use your CD as a guide to cut out a paper circle to cover one side of the CD.

Step 2: Glue the paper to the CD.

Step 3: Cut the sweet wrappers into lots of little shapes, like this.

Step 4: Stick them on the CD. Leave a little space between each piece of paper.

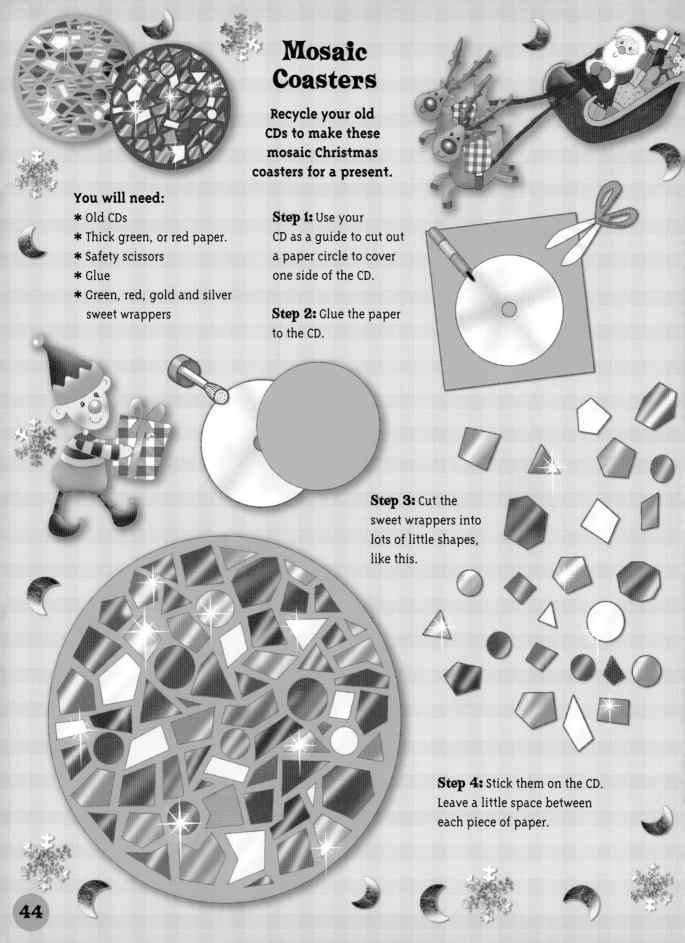

Pot Pourri Trees

These scented Christmas trees are perfect gifts for the family.

You will need:
* Tracing paper * White paper * Pencil * Safety scissors
* Scraps of fabric * Needle and thread * Ready-made pot pourri
* Buttons and beads for decoration

Step 1: Trace this tree shape onto white paper. Cut out the tree shape.

Step 2: Use the white shape as a pattern to cut out two tree shapes from the fabric.

Step 3: With the right sides of the material facing, ask an adult to help sew the two tree shapes together. Leave a small gap at the bottom — use this to turn your tree inside out.

Step 4: Use the gap to stuff your tree with pot pourri. Sew up the gap.

Step 5: Decorate your tree with buttons and beads and a loop for the top.

Happy Penguins

Make a row of happy penguins...
you could also make elves, or happy Santas!

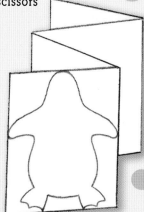

You will need:

* Piece of plain white paper about 38cm (15in) wide and 15cm (6in) high * Pencil crayons, or felt-tips * Safety scissors

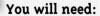

38 cm (15in)

15cm (6in)

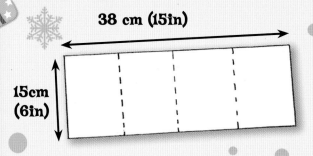

Step 2: Draw a penguin shape on the front, so that the wings and feet touch the edges of the paper.

Step 1: Fold the rectangle of white paper concertina style, so the two shorter edges meet.

Bright Baubles

Make some baubles for your Christmas tree.

You will need:

* Plain polystyrene baubles
* Poster paints
* Wool, or ribbon
* Glitter and sequins
* Old newspaper
* Needle * Glue

Step 1: Paint the polystyrene balls in bright shades. You might need a few coats to make the shades really strong.

Step 2: When the paint is dry, ask an adult to pierce a hole through the middle of each ball using a needle and some wool, or thin ribbon. Secure this with a knot, or double bow.

Step 3: Ask an adult to carefully cut this out, cutting through all the folded paper.

Step 4: Open out your chain of penguins. Using pencil crayons, or felt tips, draw their faces, wings and feet. Make each one look different.

Step 5: You can make more of these chains and join them together with sticky tape.

Step 3: Dot the balls with glue in different patterns. Try spots, stripes, or spirals and then sprinkle glitter on the glue. Shake any loose glitter onto a sheet of newspaper.

Step 4: Hang your baubles on your tree, or somewhere where they catch the light.

Stars and Angels Mobile

Use these shapes to make a coat hanger mobile.

You will need;

* Thin white card * Tracing paper
* Pencil crayons, or felt-tips
* Safety scissors
* A metal coat hanger
* Tinsel to cover the coat hanger
* Sticky tape
* String, or thin ribbon

Step 1: Trace these shapes onto the white card.

Step 2: Cut out the shapes. Decorate them with pencil crayons or felt-tips. Ask an adult to make a hole at the top of each shape.

Step 3: Wrap the tinsel around the coat hanger. If you need to, fix it on with sticky tape.

Step 4: Thread the string, or ribbon, through the hole on each shape and tie it to the coat hanger.

Pet Stockings

Make a Christmas stocking for your pet.

You will need:

* A piece of felt big enough for the stocking
* Black felt for the paw and other decoration
* Large needle
* Thread
* Scissors
* Tracing paper
* White paper
* Pencil
* Glue

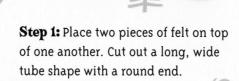

Step 1: Place two pieces of felt on top of one another. Cut out a long, wide tube shape with a round end.

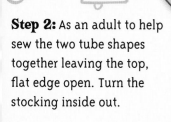

Step 2: As an adult to help sew the two tube shapes together leaving the top, flat edge open. Turn the stocking inside out.

Step 3: Cut out paw shapes from the black felt. Stick them to the 'toe' end of the stocking.

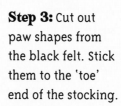

Step 4: Use one of these shapes to make a decoration for your pet's stocking. Trace it onto a piece of white paper and cut out the shape.

Step 5: Pin the shape to the black felt and cut around it.

Step 6: Glue the shape to the stocking.

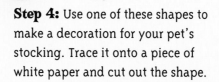

Reindeer Race

Try this game of challenges with your friends and family.

To make the counters you will need:
* Thin card – 1 A4 sheet
* Tracing paper
* Safety scissors
* Pencil crayons, or felt-tips

Trace and copy the counter 5 times onto card. Fill these in different shades and cut them out. You will need one counter for each player.

START

Close your eyes and touch the person's nose on your left.

Hop on one leg and count to 10.

Whistle for 10 seconds.

Dance on the spot for 60 seconds.

Mime eating food. Can the others guess what sort of food it is?

Say a nursery rhyme.

Make a noise like a monkey.

Say only yes or no for the rest of the game.

Pretend to be a famous singer. Can the others guess who you are?

Keep one hand behind your back for the rest of the game.

Cluck like a chicken.

Pretend to be an elephant.

Pretend to be a ballerina for 20 seconds.

50

Rules:

Make a reindeer counter for each player and find a die. Take it in turns to roll the die — the first person to get a 6 starts. Choose a path and move your counter along the path until you reach the sleigh. If you land on a challenge, you have to do what it says. The reindeer to reach the sleigh first is the winner.

END

Pretend to be a belly dancer

Do 10 star jumps

Pat your head and rub your tummy at the same time.

Pretend to hula hoop for 10 seconds.

Try to touch your nose with your tongue.

Tell a joke.

Talk about your family for 60 seconds without repeating any words.

Swap a piece of clothing with the person on your right.

Say the days of the week backwards.

Don't speak for the rest of the game unless it's to do a challenge.

Hug the person to your left.

Sing like an opera singer for 10 seconds.

Jigsaw Robins

Trace the wavy jigsaw pieces onto thin card and cut them out.

Put together the jigsaw pieces to make a picture of robins in the snow.

Christmas Photo Frames

Make this frame with a picture of you for your friends, or family.

You will need:
* Empty CD box * Photo * Safety scissors * Sticky tape * Glue
* Cardboard to fit the CD box * Paints, or felt-tips
* **Optional** - decorations for the frame

Step 1: Take out the paper inserts inside the CD box.

Step 2: Choose your photo. It will need to fit into the front of the box with about 1cm (½ in) border around the edge. The top of the picture should be at the hinged edge. Use strips of sticky tape to hold the photo in place against the plastic.

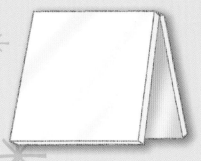

Step 3: Cut a 1cm (½in) frame out of the cardboard to fit on the front of the CD case. Draw, or paint, a pattern on the frame. Fix it to the plastic with glue.

Step 4: Use tinsel, glitter, stickers, or red ribbon to decorate the frame.

Treetop Star

Make this special star for the top of your Christmas tree.

You will need:
* Thick square piece of card * Orange, or yellow paint * Glue * Glitter
* Saucer * Pencil * Ruler * Craft knife * Green pipe cleaner

Step 1: Paint each side of the paper and let it dry.

Step 2: Place the saucer in the middle of the paper. Draw a circle round it. Use the ruler to draw 4 long lines through the middle of the circle, as shown. They should all be about the same length and distance apart.

Step 3: Draw short lines in between the long lines, as shown.

Step 4: Draw the star points as shown.

Step 5: Cut out the star.

54

Step 6: Ask an adult to help you score through all of the straight lines using a ruler and a craft knife.

Step 7: Gently pinch the long lines upwards and the short lines downwards.

Step 8: Glue the pipe cleaner to the middle of the star at the back, as shown. Twist the pipe cleaner around a pencil. Dab glue on the front of the star and sprinkle with glitter. When this is dry, do the same on the other side.

Step 9: Remove the pencil and attach your star to the top of the tree with the pipe cleaner.

Dancing Penguin

Make a dancing penguin decoration for your tree.

You will need:
* Large piece of black paper * Small plate
* Pencil * Safety scissors * Glue * White paint
* Sticky tape * String, or thin ribbon * Tracing paper

Step 1: Use a small plate to draw a circle on your paper.

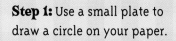

Step 2: Cut out the circle. Fold it in half. Open it out and cut along the fold. Keep the paper that's left over for later.

Step 3: Glue along the straight edge of one piece and curl the paper to make a cone. Paint, a white tummy and little feet.

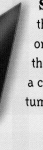

Glue

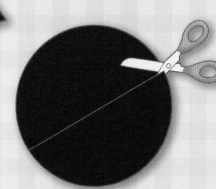

Step 4: Snip off a tiny piece of the pointed tip of the cone. Tie a loop in your piece of string or ribbon, as shown. Push the loop end through the hole in the top of the cone.

Step 5: Cut out an oval shape from the other piece of paper. Draw a penguin face.

Step 6: Stick the face to the string or ribbon, just above the body.

Use the loop to hang up your dancing penguin.

Mini Cards

Use these tiny cards as Christmas present tags, or put one into a Christmas stocking with a special message.

You will need:

* Thin card about 16x11cm (6.5x4in)
* Tracing paper * Pencil
* Pencil crayons, or felt-tips
* Safety scissors

Step 1: Fold the piece of card in half. Trace one of these pictures onto the front of the card.

Step 2: Use pencil crayons, or felt-tips to decorate the card.

Step 3: Cut around the outer edge of the shape – make sure you cut through both sides of the card. Write your message inside.

For a Christmas tag, use a dab of glue, or a piece of sticky tape, to stick the back of the card to a present.

Christmas Lanterns

Make some pretty paper lanterns to decorate your room.

You will need:

* A4 piece of thick bright paper — this will make two lanterns
* Safety scissors
* Glue * A gold pen
* Glitter and sequins
* String, or ribbon

Strip for handle

Step 1: Fold the sheet of paper in half. Cut along the fold to make two pieces.

Step 2: Fold one of the pieces in half and make cuts along the folded side, leaving about 2.5cm (1in) not cut at all, as shown.

Step 3: Cut the last strip off to make the lantern handle.

Holly Place Cards

You will need:

* A piece of green card about 12.5cm (5in) long and 3.75cm (1½in) wide
* Pencil * Safety scissors
* Silver, or gold, gel pen

Step 1: Fold the card in half and draw half a holly leaf shape. Cut out the holly leaf shape. One half will lie flat, the other will stand upright.

Step 2: Using a gold, or silver, gel pen, write each person's name on the upright part of the holly leaf.

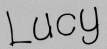

Lucy

Put your holly place cards on the table when you have your Christmas meal to show people where to sit.

Step 4: Open the piece of paper. Bend it round and glue the two ends together.

Step 5: Put a blob of glue, or sticky tape, on the two ends of the handle and press this onto the top of the lantern.

Glue

Step 6: Decorate your lantern with a gold pen, glitter, or sequins and then make some more!

Step 7: Hang your lanterns on string, or ribbon, across a corner of a room.

Pompom Heads

You will need:
* Two small pompoms
* Plain paper
* Pencils in different shades
* Safety scissors * Glue

Draw a Santa, an elf face and some hats. Cut these out. Glue them to your pompoms and decorate their faces.

Sit your pompom heads in egg cups, candlesticks, or just on a shelf.

Mrs Santa's Kitchen

Make a fun picture of Mrs Santa baking Christmas cakes for the elves.

You will need:

* Large sheet of white paper
* Lots of bits of Christmas wrapping paper
* Plain paper in different shades
* Any scraps of fabric
* Safety scissors
* Glue
* Pencil crayons, felt-tips and paints

Use the scraps of paper and fabric, pencil crayons, felt-tips, and paints to make a picture of Mrs Santa in her kitchen, like the one shown here.

Glue

Holly Cakes

Make these cookies using melted marshmallows.

You will need:

- 5 tablespoons of butter
- 20 large marshmallows
- 453g (16oz) cornflakes
- ½ teaspoon green food dye
- Small red sweets for the berries
- Cake cases

Step 1: Ask an adult to help you melt the butter. Add a few marshmallows at a time and melt these as well.

Step 2: Take the mixture off the heat. Stir in the green food dye to make it bright green, like holly.

Step 3: Gently stir in the cornflakes.

Step 4: Drop spoonfuls of the holly mixture into the cake cases. Add two or three red sweets to make the berries.

Step 5: Place them in the fridge to cool and set.

Pretty Placemats

Make festive placemats for the dinner table.

You will need:

- 1 sheet of plain A4 paper for each placemat
- Pencils, or felt-tips
- Laminating paper

Draw a Christmas picture on the paper, or make a picture using old Christmas cards or present tags. When you've finished, laminate the placemats before you use them. You can mount them on card so that they last longer.

Sparkly Card

Make this card for someone special.

You will need:

* Green paper * Safety scissors
* Red felt-tip, or pencil crayon
* Glue
* Small piece of festive
   paper for the star
* Green pipe cleaner
* Sequins, or gems

Step 1: Draw a Christmas tree on your piece of green paper. Make the tub red.

Step 2: Cut out the Christmas tree shape. Write your message on the back. Or stick the tree on a piece of card folded in half for a more traditional Christmas card.

Step 3: Bend your pipe cleaner and stick it on the front of the tree. Cut out a star from your Christmas paper and stick it on the top.

Step 4: Dab glue on the card. Stick on the sequins, or gems, to decorate your tree.

Name Cards

Make some mosaic name cards to show people where to sit for your Christmas meal.

You will need:
* ✱ Stiff white card ✱ Safety scissors ✱ Bits of plain paper in Christmas shades such as red, green, gold and silver
* ✱ Glue ✱ Felt-tips ✱ Glitter

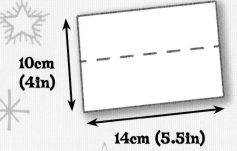

10cm (4in)

14cm (5.5in)

Step 1: For each place card, you will need to cut out a piece of card 14cm (5.5in) long by 10cm (4in) high. Draw a line halfway across. One half of the card will have a mosaic, the other half will have the person's name.

Step 2: Cut out lots of mosaic shapes to decorate your card.

Stick on mosaic shapes

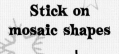

Step 3: Stick your mosaic shapes to one half of the card. Leave a small white space around each shape.

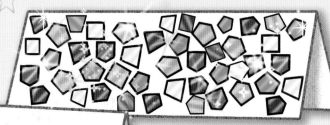

SAM

Step 4: When the card is dry, fold it in half. Use a felt-tip to write the person's name on the blank side.

Place your card on the table where the person is sitting. The name side should face the chair and the mosaic side is the table decoration.

Personal Christmas Card

A special card for your best friends.

You will need:

* Tracing paper * Pencil
* Thin card, folded from side to side
* Pencil crayons, or felt-tips
* Safety scissors * Glue
* Small photo of your head
* Glitter, or sequins, to decorate
  your card

Step 1: Trace one of these figures onto the folded card.

Step 2: Stick the photo of your head on the top.

Step 3: Use pencil crayons, felt-tips, glitter and sequins to decorate your card.

Write a fun message inside.

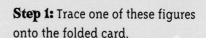

Christmas Jigsaw

Make a Christmas jigsaw for yourself,
or as a gift for a friend.

You will need:

* Pencil
* Thin card
* Pencil crayons,
  or felt-tips
* Safety scissors

Draw a Christmas
scene on thin card.
Cut it into lots of
pieces like the
shapes shown here
to make your own
Christmas jigsaw.

Elf Mask

Make these fun elf masks from paper plates.

You will need:
* One large paper plate for each mask
* Crayons, paints, or felt-tips
* Cotton wool
* Ribbon for tying on your mask

Step 1: Copy one of these masks, or make up your own elf face.

Step 2: Ask an adult to help cut out the eyes for you.

Step 3: Add cotton wool for a beard

Make an elf hat to go with your mask. Cut a paper plate from one edge to the middle. Fold it to make a cone and glue the cut edges together.

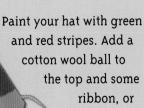

Paint your hat with green and red stripes. Add a cotton wool ball to the top and some ribbon, or elastic, to hold it on

Step 4: Ask an adult to help you make holes at each side. Thread through the ribbon and tie on your mask.

Glitter Spirals

Pretty decorations to hang on the tree, or to decorate a present.

You will need
* Plain paper in shiny red, green, silver, or gold * Pencil
* Glue * Silver and gold glitter, or red and green glitter
* Old newspaper * Thread, or thin ribbon

Step 1: Draw a spiral shape onto the paper, like this.

Step 2: Ask an adult to help you cut out the spiral. Make a hole in the top where the x is.

Step 3: Lay the spiral on old newspaper. Cover it in glue and sprinkle with glitter.

Step 4: Use the thread, or ribbon, to tie your spiral onto the tree, or on a present.

Make Your Own Christmas Cards

You will need:

✻ Blank cards and envelopes ✻ Plain paper in bright shades, or Christmas wrapping paper
✻ Pencil ✻ Safety scissors ✻ Tracing paper ✻ Glue ✻ Glitter

holly

star

stocking

snowman

candle

Step 1: Trace one of these shapes onto your paper and cut it out.

Step 2: Stick the paper shape onto the front of a blank card.

Don't forget to write a Christmas message inside your card.

Stand-up Christmas Tree

Make two or three of these little trees for a Christmas forest.

You will need:

* Piece of card folded in half from side to side * Safety scissors
* Green pencil crayon, or felt-tip
* A clean yogurt pot, or something similar
* Christmas wrapping paper to cover the pot
* Play clay * Glue, or sticky tape
* Stick on gems, sequins and glitter to decorate the tree * Tinsel

Step 1: Draw a Christmas tree on your folded card. Make both sides green.

Step 2: Cut out the trees through both pieces of card so you have two trees. Cut a slit in each tree, as shown.

Step 3: Cover your pot in wrapping paper. Use glue or sticky tape to fix it in place. Put some play clay in the bottom of the pot, to about half way up.

Step 4: Slot the two pieces of the Christmas tree together as shown.

Step 5: Fix your tree into the clay in the pot.

Step 6: Use the gems, sequins and glitter to make your tree sparkle. Put tinsel around the bottom of the tree to cover the clay.

Present Box

Make a present box for a special gift.

You will need:

* An old cardboard box with a lid
* Green, red, gold, or silver paint for the box
* Old Christmas cards, magazines, or comics
* Safety scissors
* Glue
* Glitter

Step 1: Paint the box.

Step 2: Cut out pictures from your Christmas cards, comics, or magazines to decorate your box.

Step 3: Stick the pictures on the box. Sprinkle with glitter for a festive finish.

Use your box for Christmas keepsakes, or for a special present for a friend.

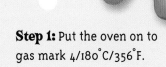

Santa Cakes

Ask an adult to help make these tasty treats.

For 12 cakes you will need:

- 100g (4oz) soft butter
- 100g (4oz) self raising flour
- 100g (4oz) caster sugar
- 2 eggs

For the decoration you will need:

- Icing sugar and water, or ready-made icing
- Chocolate drops, or raisins
- Glacé cherries
- Chocolate buttons

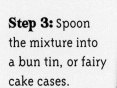

Step 1: Put the oven on to gas mark 4/180°C/356°F.

Step 2: Put all the cake ingredients into a bowl and whisk them together until creamy.

Step 3: Spoon the mixture into a bun tin, or fairy cake cases.

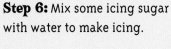

Step 4: Cook for 10-15 minutes. To check they are cooked, press gently. If the cake is springy it is cooked.

Step 5: Place the cakes on a wire tray and let them cool.

Step 6: Mix some icing sugar with water to make icing.

Step 7: Use a small spoon to add an icing beard and hair to your Santa cakes. Add chocolate drops, or raisins, for eyes, a glacé cherry for his nose and chocolate buttons for cheeks.

Party Bags

Here are some ways to make plain party bags look festive.

To Holly
Merry
Christmas

Stick on pipe cleaners in the shape of Christmas trees, and paper holly shapes, for a festive 3D effect. Use beads, stick-on gems, or buttons, for the berries.

Use felt-tips to write on the person's name. Go over the name with glue and then sprinkle with gold, or silver, glitter. Tie a red ribbon in a bow and glue it on the bag.

To my best friend

To make your gift bag personal, stick on a picture of yourself, or a friend. Add a speech bubble with a message. Draw on Christmas patterns to finish.

Cut out Christmas pictures from old cards and magazines and cover the bag to make a montage.

Christmas Crown

Make your own crown this Christmas.

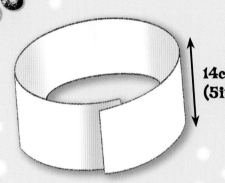

You will need:

* Thin card wide enough to fit around your head * Safety scissors
* Pencil crayons, or felt-tips * Sequins, stickers, stick-on jewels, or glitter, to decorate

14cm (5in)

Step 1: Cut out a length of card wide enough to fit around your head and overlap slightly. It should be about 14cm (5in) deep.

Step 2: Draw triangles to make your crown. Use your pencil crayons, or felt-tips, to make it look gold. Cut it out.

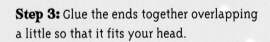

Step 3: Glue the ends together overlapping a little so that it fits your head.

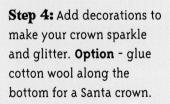

Step 4: Add decorations to make your crown sparkle and glitter. **Option** - glue cotton wool along the bottom for a Santa crown.

Make some counters, find a die, and then
see who can reach the fireplace first.

To make the counters you will need:

* Thin card –
  1 A4 sheet
* Tracing paper
* Safety scissors
* Felt-tips

Trace or copy the shapes onto the card. Fill them in and cut them out. You will need one counter for each player.

END

START

76

Rules:

The first person to throw a six starts. Take it in turns to throw the die and move your counter around the board. When you land on the bottom of a chimney, you climb up. When you land on the top, you slide down. The first person to reach the fireplace is the winner.

Sparkly Icicles

You will need:
* Sparkly pipe cleaners
* Thread

Step 1: Carefully twist a pipe cleaner round in a flat spiral.

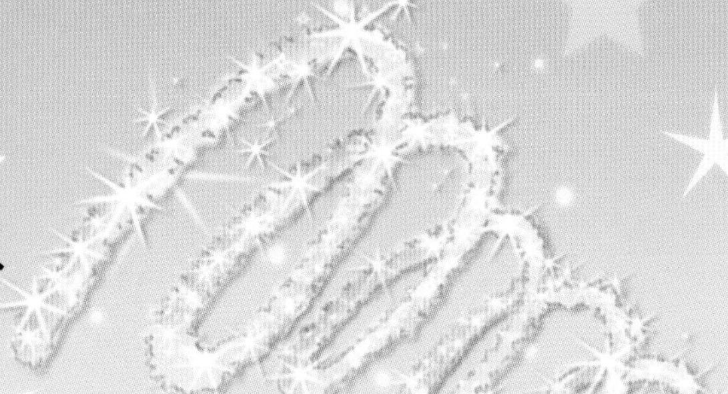

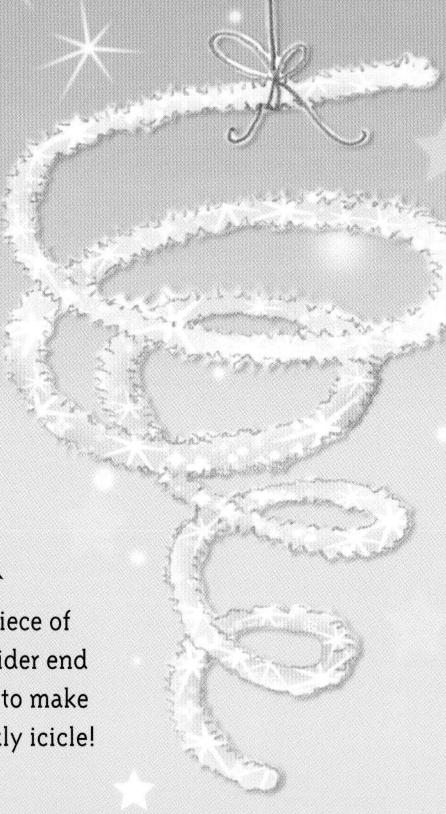

Step 2: Hold the two ends and gently pull, so that the spiral stretches out.

Step 3: Tie a piece of thread to the wider end and hang it up to make a dangly, sparkly icicle!

Pop-up Santa Card

You will need:

* A sheet of thick A4 card * A smaller piece of paper to fit inside the card
* Pencil crayons, or paint * Glue

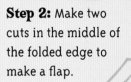

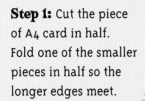

Step 1: Cut the piece of A4 card in half. Fold one of the smaller pieces in half so the longer edges meet.

Step 2: Make two cuts in the middle of the folded edge to make a flap.

Step 3: Open out the folded piece of card and pinch the flap, so it folds inside the card like a step.

Step 4: Close the card with the flap folded inside. Fold the other piece of card in half and glue this to the back of the first piece.

Step 5: Cut out a separate piece of paper, small enough to fit inside the card.

Step 6: Draw Santa going down a chimney on this smaller piece of paper.

Step 7: Paint, or draw, a night sky on one half of the inside of your card and roof tiles on the bottom half.

Step 8: Cut out your Santa and chimney and glue this onto the step inside your card. Fold it and unfold it to make sure it works.

Christmas Badges

These Christmas badges are great stocking fillers, or put one into a Christmas card for a fun surprise.

Step 1: Choose which badge you want to make. Trace and copy the shape onto the card.

You will need:
* Tracing paper
* Pencil
* Pencil crayons, or felt-tips
* Thin card
* Sticky tape
* Safety pin

Step 2: Use your felt-tips, or pencil crayons, to finish the picture on one side of the badge. Next, cut out the shape.

Step 3: Use a piece of sticky tape to fix a safety pin to the back of the badge.

For a very special badge, draw one of these frames onto white card. Stick a picture of you, or your family, in the middle. Perfect for friends, or family, who live a long way away.

Christmas Candles

Make these pretty candles for the Christmas table.

For each candle you will need:
* Sheet of paper about A4 * Saucer, or small plate
* A pair of safety scissors * Glue * Pencil crayons,
  or felt-tips * Glitter, or sequins, to decorate

Step 1: Fold the paper
in half from top to bottom.
Use a saucer or plate to draw
a semicircle on one side.

Step 2: Cut out the
semicircle and fill it in.

Step 3: Draw a
flame shape onto
the left over paper.
Cut out the flame
and make it red.

Step 4: Put a little glue
at the bottom of the
flame and stick it to the
middle of the semicircle.

Add sequins, or glitter, to finish your Christmas candle.

Thumbprint Robins

You will need:
* Red paint * Paper * A paintbrush
* Brown paint * A black felt-tip

Step 1: Dip your thumb into some red paint.

Step 2: Press your thumb on a piece of paper several times. Leave a space between each thumbprint.

Step 3: Using a paintbrush, paint a brown oval and wings round each red thumbprint.

Step 4: Leave these to dry. Then, with your black felt-tip, draw the robin's eyes, beak and legs. Try to make each robin look different.

Christmas Tree Fairies

Make a pretty fairy for the top of your tree.

You will need:
* 2 sheets of white paper
* A plate that fits on the paper
* A sparkly pipe cleaner
* Safety scissors
* Glue, or sticky tape
* Glitter and paint
* 1 bead for the head

Step 1: Draw round the plate on a sheet of paper so you have a semicircle.

Step 2: Cut out the semicircle.

Step 3: Curve the semicircle to make a cone. Glue, or tape, the straight edges together. This is the fairy's body.

Magic Painting

Use this special way of painting, called wax resist, to make a snowy, night-time scene.

You will need:
* A large sheet of white paper
* A white wax crayon, or white candle
* Dark blue poster paints

Step 1: On the large sheet of white paper, use the white wax crayon, or white candle, to draw a picture of a snowman on a snowy winter's night. Everything you draw with this will stay white.

Step 2: Paint over all the paper with dark blue paint. The wax will resist the paint and your picture will appear, like magic!

Step 4: Fold the other piece of paper in half and draw a wing on one side by the fold. Cut out to make a pair of wings. Add glitter, or paint.

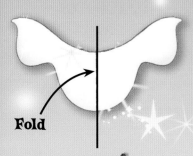

Fold

Step 5: Glue the wings onto the back of the fairy's body.

Step 6: Push the bead onto a sparkly pipe cleaner. Twist the top of the pipe cleaner to keep the bead in place and make a halo.

Step 7: Push the pipe cleaner through the cone.

Your fairy is ready to fly to the top of the tree!

Christmas Masks

Make these masks of Santa and Rudolph for your
Christmas party, or make up a Christmas play.

You will need:

* 20cm (8in) square of paper
* Tracing paper * Pencil
* Thin ribbon, or wool
* Pencils, or felt-tips
* Safety scissors

Step 1: Fold your
piece of paper in half.
Trace a Santa or
Rudolph face onto it
as shown, or draw
your own mask.

Step 2: Cut out
the mask shape.

Step 3: Open out the mask and fill it in. Ask an adult to help you cut out holes for the eyes. Hold the mask against your face. Make a pencil mark where your eyes are. Ask an adult to help cut out holes.

Step 4: Ask an adult to help you make a small hole at each side. Thread a piece of ribbon, or wool, through each hole.

Step 5: Tie on the mask and play.

Christmas Pizza

Make this tasty festive pizza for a party.

You will need:

- A ready-made pizza base with tomato sauce
- Cheese square slices
- 1 tomato
- 2 or 3 mushrooms
- Green and red pepper
- Pineapple chunks
- Slices of chorizio sausage

Step 1: Cut triangles from the cheese slices. Put them in the middle of the pizza to make the Christmas tree. If your pizza is big enough, do two trees.

Step 2: Ask an adult to help you cut a tomato and the mushrooms into small pieces to make the tree decorations.

Step 3: Ask an adult to help you slice the peppers into thin strips.

Step 4: Decorate your tree using the mushroom and tomato pieces as baubles and the pepper strips as tinsel.

Step 5: Decorate the edge of your pizza with the chunks of pineapple.

Step 6: Cut a slice of sausage into a star and place it on the top of the tree. Cut another slice into a tub shape.

Cook, eat and enjoy!

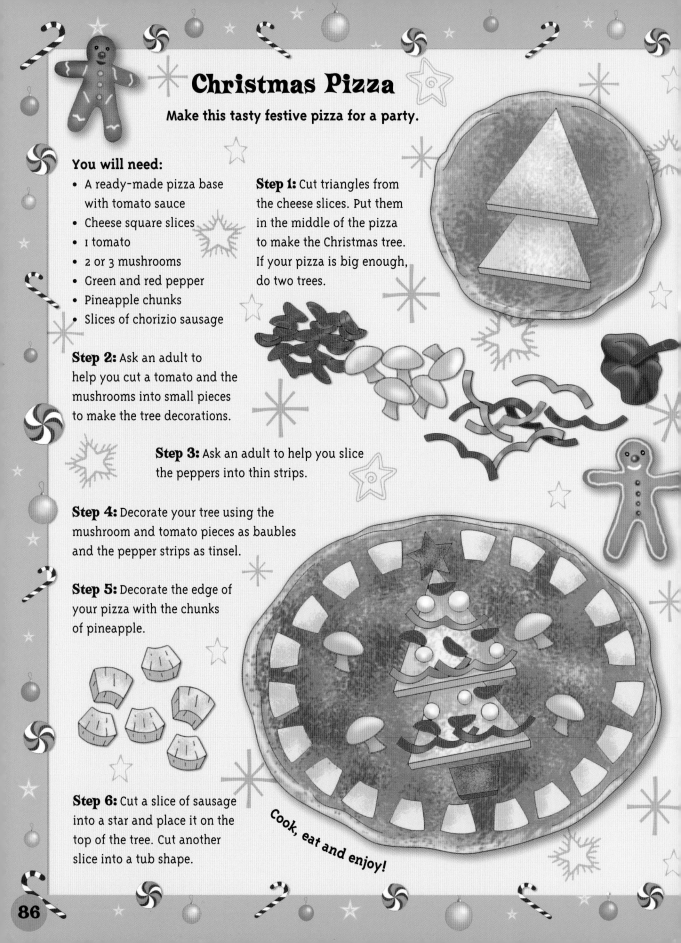

Guess the Gift

A hilarious party game for all the family.

To play, draw a present on a piece of paper. Here are some ideas:

Fold the pieces of paper and put them in a box. Each person picks one and has to act out what the gift is without making any sounds. The person to guess the gift picks the next gift to mime.

Chocolate Truffles

Mouth-watering truffles to share with friends and family.

You will need:

- Bar of chocolate
- 1 tablespoon of butter
- 2 tablespoons (30ml) of whipped cream
- Drinking chocolate powder, or coconut flakes

Step 1: Ask an adult to help you melt the chocolate in a bowl over a pan of boiling water.

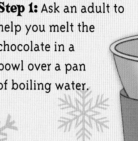

Step 2: Take the bowl off the pan. Stir in the, butter and cream.

Step 3: Whisk the mixture until it is thick. Put it in the fridge to chill for about an hour.

Step 4: To make the truffle balls, scoop out a tablespoon of the mixture. Shape the mix into a ball. Roll the balls in drinking chocolate powder, or coconut flakes.

To give the truffles as a present, wrap them in pretty paper and tie with a red or green, bow.

Sparkly Stars

Make some twinkling stars for your Christmas tree, or as gift tags.

You will need:
* Card in bright shades * Safety scissors
* Glue * Glitter * Newspaper
* A hole punch * Ribbon

Step 1: Draw some large stars on a piece of card and cut them out.

Step 2: Cover one side with glue and sprinkle with glitter. When this is dry, shake any loose glitter onto the newspaper. Add glitter to the other side.

Step 3: Using a hole punch, make a hole in one of the points of each star.

Step 4: Tie some ribbon through the stars and hang them up, or use them as gift labels.

Felt Finger Puppets

Make some fun festive finger puppets.

You will need:

* White paper * Pencil * Scraps of felt such as red and pink
* Safety scissors * Needle and thread * Marker pens
* Fabric glue * Extra felt and cotton wool for decoration

Step 1: Copy these figures, or make your own, on a piece of white paper.

Step 2: Use the paper shapes as a pattern to cut out two shapes from the felt. Make sure the shapes will fit your finger.

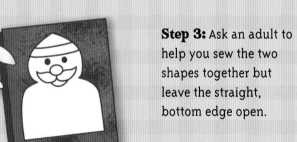

Step 3: Ask an adult to help you sew the two shapes together but leave the straight, bottom edge open.

Step 4: For a Santa, cut out a circle from the pink felt. Draw on a face. Add blobs of glue along his chin, under his nose and the edge of his hat. Stick on some small bits of cotton wool.

Step 5: Cut out small bits of felt for buttons and a belt.

Christmas Recipe Book

Collect all your best Christmas recipes together.

You will need:

* Sheets of A4 paper –as many as you need for the book
* Safety scissors
* Thick paper for the cover
* Pencil crayons and felt-tips
* Long piece of ribbon
* **Optional** - camera

Step 1: Fold the sheets of paper in half.

Step 2: Cut the sheets of paper in half along the folds to make your book pages.

Step 3: Make the cut sheets of paper into a pile. Using a hole punch, make holes in the sheets. You may need to do this in lots of small piles, but try and get the holes in the same place on all the sheets of paper.

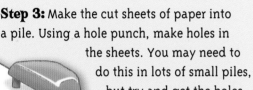

Step 4: Cut the cover paper in half and make holes. Write the title of the book and your name on the cover. Decorate it with felt-tips, or pencil crayons.

Step 5: Put all the pages inside the cover. Thread the ribbon through the holes so the two ends are at the front of the book and tie them together.

Step 6: Photograph your best food, or draw pictures. Stick them in the book.

Step 7: Underneath, write the ingredients and how to cook the food. Say whose recipe this is, or who likes it the best.

Gingerbread Men Card

Use felt to make this must-touch Christmas card.

You will need;

* White paper * Safety scissors * Pencil
* Piece of green, card about 30cm long x 14cm tall (12x5.5in) when folded * Piece of brown felt the same size as the card
* Wiggly eyes * Little strips of ribbon for collars
* Fabric glue * Stickers to finish

Step 1: Draw a gingerbread man on the white paper. Make sure it fits on your card. Cut it out.

Step 2: Use the white paper shape as a guide to cut out 4 gingerbread men from the felt, or as many as will fit in a row along your card.

Step 3: Glue the gingerbread men onto the card in a row. Add eyes to each of them

Step 4: Cut out small strips of ribbon to make a collar or bow tie for each figure.

Add stickers to finish your card.

CD Decorations

Recycle your old CDs to make these Christmas decorations.

You will need:
* Recycled CDs
* Green, or red, card
* Felt-tips
* Safety scissors
* Glue
* Old Christmas cards
* Tinsel
* Thread

Step 1: Using your CD as a guide, cut out a circle of card. Glue this onto the CD.

Step 2: Decorate your CD - you can draw a picture in the middle of the card, or cut out a picture from an old Christmas card.

Step 3: Glue tinsel around the outside of the CD.

Step 4: Ask an adult to use a strong craft hole puncher to make a hole at the top of the CD. Thread thin ribbon, or tinsel through the hole to hang it up.

Waiting for Santa

Make this picture for your room, or school.

You will need:
* Large sheet of white paper
* Lots of old magazines and comics
* Safety scissors
* Glue

Get your sheet of blank paper. Make a picture like this one using cut out pictures from comics and magazines.

See if you can find a picture of a boy sleeping, an armchair, a table with a lamp, and windows with curtains.

Put the nose on Rudolph

Trace Rudolph's nose onto a piece of card and make it red. Take it in turns to close your eyes and see who can put Rudolph's nose in the right place.

Rudolph's nose